ANTARCTICA

Alexis Roumanis

LET'S READ
AV²
BY WEIGL™
ADDED VALUE • AUDIO VISUAL

AV² provides enriched content that supplements and complements this book. Weigl's AV² book strive to create inspired learning and engage young minds in a total learning experience.

Your AV² Media Enhanced books come alive with...

Audio
Listen to sections of the book read aloud.

Video
Watch informative video clips.

Embedded Weblinks
Gain additional information for research.

Try This!
Complete activities and hands-on experiments.

Key Words
Study vocabulary, and complete a matching word activity.

Quizzes
Test your knowledge.

Slide Show
View images and captions, and prepare a presentation.

... and much, much more!

Go to **www.av2books.com**, and enter this book's unique code.

BOOK CODE

F727692

AV² by Weigl brings you media enhanced books that support active learning.

Published by AV² by Weigl
350 5th Avenue, 59th Floor New York, NY 10118
Websites: www.av2books.com   www.weigl.com

Library of Congress Cataloging-in-Publication Data

Roumanis, Alexis.
 Antarctica / Alexis Roumanis.
     pages cm. -- (Exploring continents)
 Includes bibliographical references and index.
 ISBN 978-1-4896-3026-1 (hard cover : alk. paper) -- ISBN 978-1-4896-3027-8 (soft cover : alk. paper) --
 ISBN 978-1-4896-3028-5 (single user ebook) -- ISBN 978-1-4896-3029-2 (multi-user ebook)
 1. Antarctica--Juvenile literature. I. Title.
 G863.R68 2014
 919.89--dc23
                                    2014044122

Printed in the United States of America in Brainerd, Minnesota
1 2 3 4 5 6 7 8 9 0 18 17 16 15 14

122014   Project Coordinator: Jared Siemens
WEP051214   Design: Mandy Christiansen

Weigl acknowledges iStock and Getty Images as the primary image suppliers for this title.

ANTARCTICA

Contents

Welcome to Antarctica.
It is the third smallest continent.

This is the shape
of Antarctica.
All other continents
are north of Antarctica.

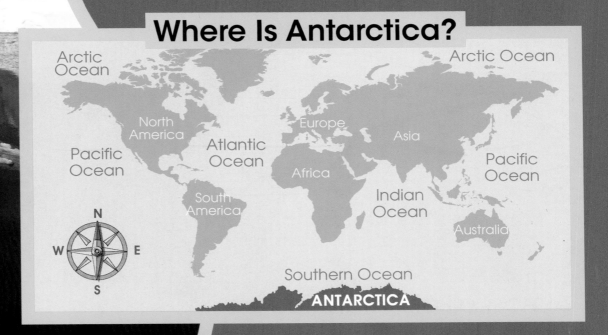

Where Is Antarctica?

Arctic Ocean

Arctic Ocean

North America

Europe

Asia

Pacific Ocean

Atlantic Ocean

Africa

Pacific Ocean

South America

Indian Ocean

Australia

N

W   E

S

Southern Ocean

ANTARCTICA

Only one ocean touches
the coast of Antarctica.

Antarctica is made up of many different landforms. Deserts, mountains, and plains can all be found in Antarctica.

Antarctica is the largest polar desert on Earth.

Almost all of Antarctica is covered in ice.

Mount Erebus is the most active volcano in Antarctica.

Vinson Massif is the tallest mountain in Antarctica.

The Ross Ice Shelf is the world's biggest piece of floating ice.

Antarctica is home to some of the most unique animals in the world. Many of these animals live in the waters around Antarctica.

Orcas can live for about 80 years.

The emperor penguin is the largest penguin in the world.

Antarctica is home to different types of plants. It is too cold for trees to grow in Antarctica.

Moss is the largest type of land plant on Antarctica.

Lichen grows about 0.4 inches (1 centimeter) every 100 years.

Red algae can grow on snow or ice in Antarctica.

Seaweed grows in the waters around Antarctica.

Grass only grows in some parts of Antarctica.

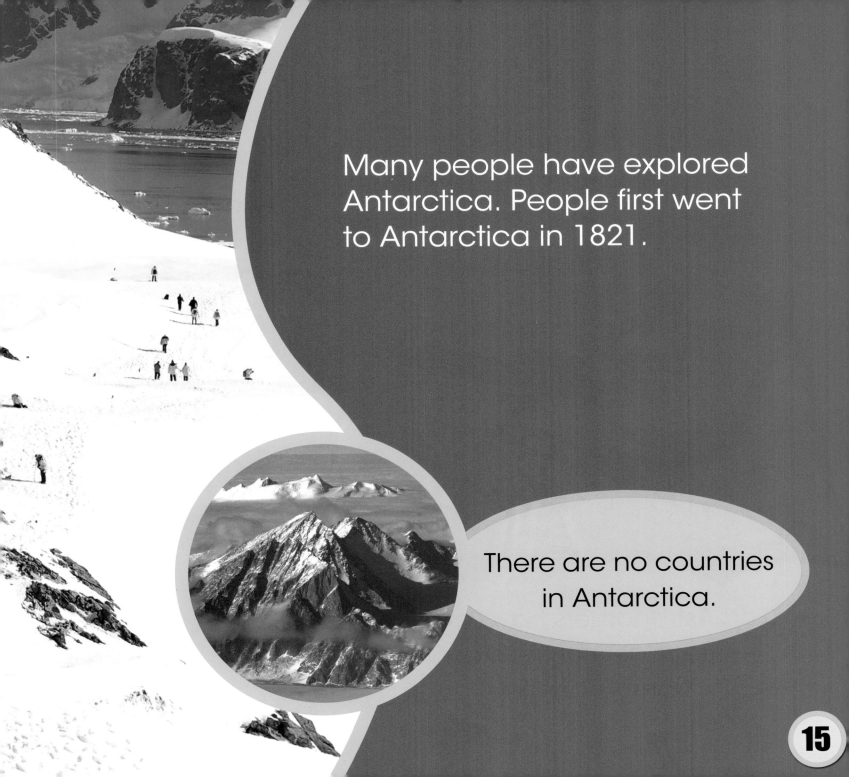

Many people have explored Antarctica. People first went to Antarctica in 1821.

There are no countries in Antarctica.

People who work in Antarctica need to have special skills. They use their skills to learn more about Antarctica.

Photographers take pictures of the land and animals.

Astronomers have a great view of the stars from Antarctica.

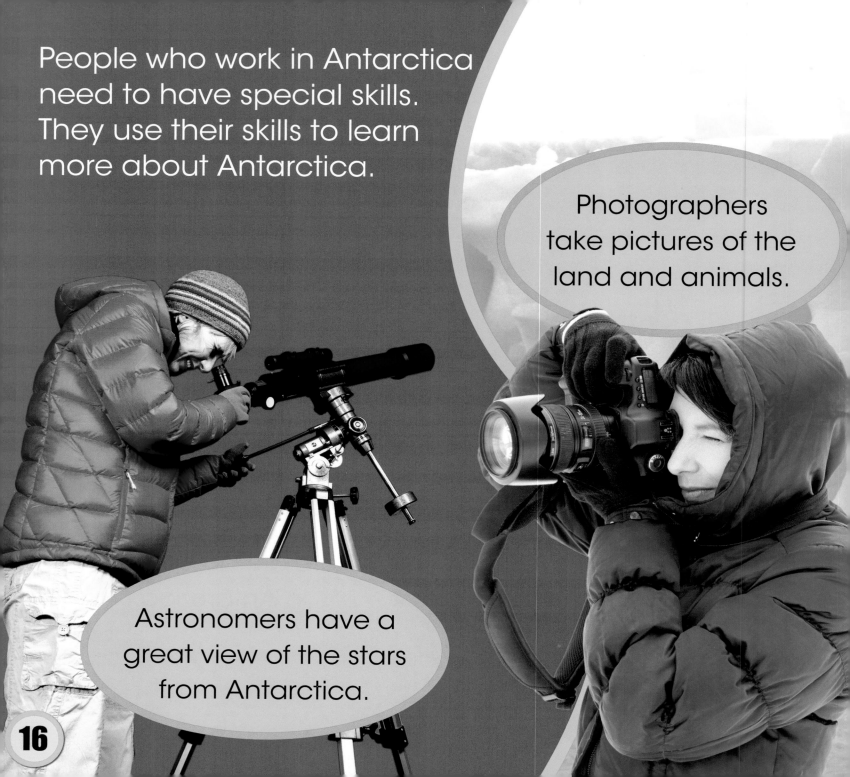

16

Around 4,400 people work in Antarctica in the summer. Most people only live there for a short time.

The largest work camp in Antarctica is McMurdo Station.

There are many things that can be found only in Antarctica.
People come from all over the world to visit this continent.

Less than 200 people spend the whole year at the South Pole.

People can go camping in Antarctica.

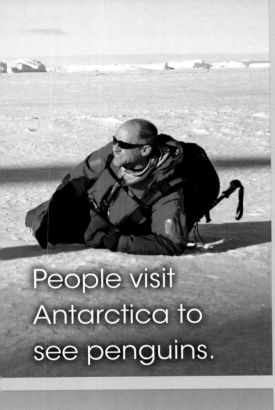

People visit Antarctica to see penguins.

Tourists can take a cruise ship to see Antarctica.

Helicopter tours are a popular way to see Antarctica from the air.

Antarctica Quiz

See what you have learned
about the continent
of Antarctica.

What do these pictures tell you
about Antarctica?

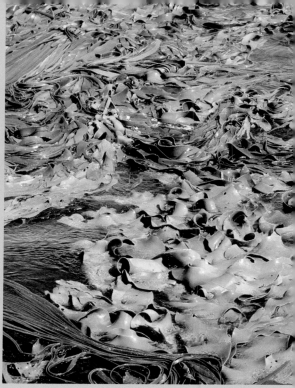

22

23

KEY WORDS

Research has shown that as much as 65 percent of all written material published in English is made up of 300 words. These 300 words cannot be taught using pictures or learned by sounding them out. They must be recognized by sight. This book contains 81 common sight words to help young readers improve their reading fluency and comprehension. This book also teaches young readers several important content words, such as proper nouns. These words are paired with pictures to aid in learning and improve understanding.

Page	Sight Words First Appearance
4	is, it, the, to
7	all, are, of, one, only, other, this, where
8	almost, and, be, can, different, Earth, found, in, made, many, most, mountains, on, up
9	world
10	a, any, for, has, two, under, very, water
11	about, animals, around, home, live, some, these, years
12	every, grow, land, or, plants, too, trees
13	parts
15	first, have, no, people, there, went
16	from, great, learn, more, need, pictures, take, their, they, use, who, work
17	study
19	time
20	at, come, go, over, see, than, that, things
21	air, way

Page	Content Words First Appearance
4	Antarctica, continent
7	coast, ocean, shape
8	deserts, ice, landforms, plains, volcano
9	piece
10	bird, elephant seals, gentoo penguin, swimmer, wandering albatross, wingspan
11	emperor penguin, orcas
12	algae, lichen, moss, snow
13	grass, seaweed
15	countries
16	astronomers, photographers, skills, stars
17	glaciologists, marine biologists, Southern Ocean
19	McMurdo Station, summer
20	camping, South Pole
21	cruise ship, helicopter, tourists, tours

Check out www.av2books.com for activities, videos, audio clips, and more!

 Go to www.av2books.com.

 Enter book code. F727692

 Fuel your imagination online!

www.av2books.com